Peaces of Me

Paula Weber

BookLeaf Publishing

Presentation by *BookLeaf Publishing*

Web: www.bookleafpub.com

E-mail: info@bookleafpub.com

ISBN: 9789357440233

First edition 2023

Dear Dad,

*Check this out! A book! An actual published
book!*

*Dedicated to my family, never forget you can
get there and that I love you, and to the many
people throughout my life who choose to inspire
others or spark creativity. It is because of you
the world goes round.*

ACKNOWLEDGEMENT

I found a writing challenge and chose to take it! I have always wanted to write and share and this challenge gave me that opportunity! I am beyond excited and thankful! It is the month of my birthday and this is how I am celebrating 42 trips around the sun. My dad always wanted to be published, we shared that dream. So here is where I begin to tell you his story. Read on!

PREFACE

Welcome to my pages. I hope that as you turn them, you appreciate them as much as I do. Amongst these pages you will find a gathering of words that are as random as me. Here you will meet the characters I live amongst and learn to love them. I hope to show you a bit of what my world is like, and I warn you, it may be scary. Seriously, I'm a pretty normal person who enjoys many things and would like to share them with the world so here we go!

Making Room

I decided to challenge myself, in more than one way.
There is of course some things that need to go, and some that need to stay.

I have no use for people in my life who lie, and truly just do not care.
So goodbye to ya'll; I hope you find yourself someday, somehow, somewhere.

I also have got no room for negativity.
All that shit does is hold my happy self in captivity.

Bring on all the challenges that will make me strong.
Let all of my days play out like a song.

A song that truly speaks to my soul.
One that lets me fall in love with all of the small things that keep me humble and whole.

Come with me

Let's adventure out,
And find somewhere to explore.
Off to find a waterfall!

Soul Full

Sunrise.sunset. The in-betweens. All of the small things. Morning dew. A calm morning by the lake. The call of a loon. A peaceful evening. Music. Magic. Mountains. Rushing water. A sandy beach. Mother nature. The song of a bird. A beautiful animal. Silence. Creativity. Painting. Sewing. Reading. Writing. Dreaming. A whisper in the wind. Sunshine. Bare feet. Laughing uncontrollably. The look of a fresh snowfall. The many shapes of snowflakes. Being free. A smile. A touch. A heartfelt conversation. Fishing. best friends. Cuddling the dog. Getting lost. The sound of a steady rain. Dancing in the car, and then dancing in the rain. A spark. Being a light. Kindness. Being random. Camping. True human connections. An absolute love. A child's laugh. Sitting by a fire. Counting stars. Make your soul full.

Dad

A lover of science fiction,
And all things astronomy.
Someday we will live on Mars,
He truly believed.

If there was weary weather on the way,
He could be found on a porch
Watching the storms roll in.
Something in the stir of mother nature lit him
like a torch.

He was a master at life's advice.
He had his own funny ways,
To make sense of the nonsense,
Even though he sounded a bit crazed some days.

"Always listen to the good doctor."
Meaning Doctor Suess.
"Pay attention, he knows what he is talking
about."
That was a man that to him was not obtuse.

Music, a passion of his.
He loved the songs of the storytelling greats.
I can still picture him belting out all his tunes,
And often telling stories of their various fates.

Working on cars and mechanics was a thing.
He used the tools that were his dads
To make sure we knew what to do,
And teach us to not be afraid to work with our
hands.

He never said I love you.
He had his own ways.
His was to say I am proud of you.
Until the end of his days.

My Mind is a Madhouse

My pen is lost, I cannot write.
Oh crap now what do I do?
I love sunsets, they are the most beautiful sight.
Shit, my shoelace broke and I can't tie my shoe!

That pile of dishes in the kitchen sink,
It's become quite a messy pile and quite large.
I'm not sure I like the color pink.
Sometimes I really want to know who's in
charge.

The bathroom needs cleaning, especially the
shower.
I think I left some things unfinished at work.
Life is exhausting, let's go to happy hour.
Today some guy flipped me off, what a jerk!

My mind is always all over the place.
I'm sometimes amazed if I can make it through
an entire day with grace.

Flash the light

Shine your flashlight in someone's tunnel and
take a peek inside.
Please don't just walk by.
Be the light in their dark that they may need.
Help water their seed.
You may save their life instead of it becoming
too late to hear their cry.

That's me!

I am that loud, boisterous one in the crowd.
Here to make you laugh so you don't feel down.

Meet Chris- His Later Years

My dad was an alcoholic.
There is no other way to say that, no way around
it.

It is sad to see someone you love most
deteriorate, and drink away everything he had.
Eventually all he had left was his shelf of books,
his truck, and the shirt on his back.

He asked for help from us, his adult children, he
needed a place to stay.
He couldn't see he needed to quit, so we turned
him away.

That was one of the hardest things I ever had to
do, turn my own dad away.
My words to him were, "Dad, you're
grandchildren don't deserve to see you this way."

He then dissapeared a for a few weeks.
When he returned to me, he had fear in his
voice, and tears down his cheeks.

He said to me, "PJ you're right. I can't do this
anymore. Please take me to rehab."
I did all the research, and made some calls, then
said okay let's go dad.

My oldest brother and I got into dad's truck and
drove him there,checked him in, and then
walked out the door.
What came next was up to him, nothing more.

He spent that first week going through some bad
withdrawals.
Also a ton of testing, and doctor calls.

I recall him telling me something that scared
him bad was watching a young man on heroin
violently seize for days.
He said that was it, he could not imagine ever
being that way.

There was a lot of trauma he blocked out over
his life.
Losing his dad when he was seven made for a
lot of strife.

Rehab helped him learn he could not keep things
in forever.
It helped him find ways to really begin to heal,
not that he wasn't clever.

For four years after he lived with me.
He felt safest here with us, so he would not go
out for fear he had of keeping the wrong
company.

As time passed he learned to use the computer.
He began socializing online, then met Leslie,
yup it was her.

It was her he would confide and find comfort in,
and learn to live free.
So he left wisconsin for the very first time in his
life, and took his beloved cat twinkie, off to the
Foothills of the Smoky mountains in East
Tennessee.

It Happens All of the Time

I did it again, I tripped on my shoelaces.
While walking through life and then running the
bases.
I hit the ground face down, splat!
Why in the hell did I do that?
I blame my unsteady homeostasis.

This Guy...

Conversations around our home
Always result in something punny.
I swear to you, this guy.
He always thinks he's so damn funny.

In all honesty,
I would not trade him for the world.
He is the person I can't do life without,
Even if his puns make me roll my eyes and say I
want to hurl.

He does his part around the house,
And helps pay the bills.
He never misses a moment to tell me how much
he loves me.
Most of all he holds everything together when
my world feels all downhill.

He dealt with my kids when he didn't have to.
They were pre-teens when he stepped in.
You can imagine they did not make it all easy.
There were definitely times he probably wanted
to throw them into a garbage bin.

We do life together.
The ups and downs and in betweens.
And most who know us,
Probably think we are the weirdest couple they
have ever seen.

We randomly road trip,
And do whatever we feel like that day.
That is just how we do it.
It is how we pass the time away.

He puts up with all my crazy ideas,
And sometimes even helps.
What more could a girl ask for with a partner in
crime.
Except maybe someday to take me to the Swiss
Alps.

My Dad...to This Guy

My daughter is fierce and she knows her place.
Don't you dare make her unhappy,
because she will retaliate,
And possibly wipe that smile right off your face.

She is determined and strong.
She can make anything happen.
She is a super human,
And in my eyes she is never wrong.

You want to be with her,
Well just be prepared.
She has, in her corner, her two brothers and dear
old dad.
I'll warn you though, she does not really need us
sir.

You want to marry her you say.
Well you don't need my blessing,
Just my condolences.
She is a hell of a lot to handle so consider
yourself privileged if she says wants you to stay.

Breathe

Inhale,
Exhale, and then
Look around and see all
The small things. Know they matter.
Just Breathe.

Chris's Peace

A small trailer with a back porch for sitting.
He didn't need more, are you kidding?

Tucked into the mountains,
He would sit on the porch and watch the blue
fog lift like curtains.

To him, he had everything.
A sober life he was happy with, that made him
again want to write and sing.

He and Leslie, they had their talents.
They used those talents to give their life balance.

In Newport, Tennessee, on the side of Highway
twenty-five,
You could find them selling their many picked
and refurbished treasures to make the little bit of
money they needed to get by.

Sure, like any couple, they had their spats.
They always made things work for each other,
and their beloved cats.

Their cats were their kids, it started with only a few.
Then one had kittens they could not turn away, so they kept the whole brood.

Dad would message and call often, write in his blogs, and hop onto social media to check up on all of us.
He always had something smart assy to say like, " Hey PJ, did you ride the short bus?"

He didn't miss a beat keeping up with the grandkids.
He was always cheering them on for everything they did.

Time went on, 9 years, then one day I observed, He had suddenly not been saying much, and I knew something was about to take a curve.

Meet Maynard

He is extremely frumpy and has absolutely no
grace.
He also has no respect at all for personal space.
He loves to use his big ass paws to play and
clobber.
When he shakes his head there is nothing at all
safe from his slobber.
He is my one hundred pound purebred boxer
who's absolutely nuts, has my heart, and doesn't
belong any other place.

Insanity Brings Me Sanity

My sanity lies in the midst of the craziest roaring
thunder and pounding rain.
I take it in and let it wash away all of the
thoughts and worries in my brain.
It awes me to just sit and feel the depth of what
can take place is chaos.
To witness mother nature create room for new
growth on so many different levels, like a boss.
These are the moments where I leave behind the
insane.

Chris- Not His Last Chapter

Something dad would always tell me was that he was just fine.
"There is no need to uproot your life for mine."

We were on the phone and he tells me his legs feel weak today.
He describes needing to hold on to things as he walks and says he just feels like they are just going to give way.

He then describes that he has this pain in his neck and his shoulders.
He also has a cough and said it feels like sitting on his chest, is a giant boulder.

Something about him is he had this true fear of seeing a doctor alone.
So he tells me he thinks he should probably go and asks me if I'm good to leave home.

A few hours later, he calls.
He tells me he fell and is "taking an ambulance ride to the hospital."

Of course I knew already that something was
wrong.
I discussed time off with work, and then picked
up my little brother to come along.

Somewhere amidst all of this, my dad panicked
about being in a hospital alone.
He then checked himself out before getting an
MRI and got himself a ride home.

When we arrived in Tennessee we could not
believe what we could see.
My dad had lost the use of his legs completely.

There was no wheelchair or ramp involved to
move him around.
We made do with what we had until we could
figure out how to keep him safe and sound.

He was loaned a wheelchair from a friend and
my brother and I would get him where he
needed.
One would lift and the other would make sure
everything was good and put things together
where he was needing to be seated.

We did this for the bathroom, we washed him up
and got him dressed every day.

All the while trying to navigate a system in
which if you have no insurance means here you
sit and wait.

Within this week's time we got him to a doctor
and began to navigate what was next and where.
We had many people that helped to get us there.

We got him in to get an MRI,and though he did
not want to, he was going to do it this time.
I picked him up and put him on the gurney
myself and told him it will be fine.

That one showed what they said they thought
was a back injury.
Something they thought could be fixed with a
surgery.

At this point my brother needed to come home.
So my friends came to help dad so that he was
not alone.

A few days went by and things were not well.
So I made a call and told my dad he had to go
back, he was not happy with me of course, I
could tell.

We had done paperwork before I left so I had
Power of attorney.

This way I could communicate with the nurses
and doctors and he could not lie to me.

More testing was done and it was determined
that he had a large mass in his chest and in his
back some.
They were sure it was cancer and helped me
make a plan for what was going to come.

Seven weeks from beginning to end.
The entire scenario seemed to unreal, like it
should be pretend.

I spent my days on phones with doctors and
nurses and social workers from 830 miles away.
Navigating everything day by day.

Dad would text and call every day and always
send the name of a song.
The name of the song is how he was feeling that
day or about how shit always went wrong.

The amount of indescribable everything that
comes with all of this is too hard for me to
express.
It was an absolute, unbelievable, chaotic mess.

A mess that in the end my brothers and I had to
help my father decide.

We had to help him decide if he could fight to live or if he needed to accept he may die.

Chris- In (His) Hurried Frenzy

Hello.
It's good to be here.
Oh no!
I must leave now,
And continue my journey
To nowhere.
Goodbye.
Maybe we'll meet again.
Somewhere.
After I return,
From nowhere.
Goodbye.

It's What I Do

I talk to the sky
The moon and the stars above
It's a thing I do

It Wasn't His Last Chapter

Here is how I see it.
His book was closed.
He told us this could not be his last chapter.
He is right. I suppose.

You see, us kids continue on.
We are raising our own families.
We promised to share the stories.
This way, him in us they will always see.

There is a lot about my father I learned way later
on.
The things he always cherished made more
sense.
Nothing was ever perfect.
Nothing is ever meant to have that perfect white
picket fence.

We go through many trials and tribulations.
For him they were called "life lessons."
In the end, he learned from us.
He tells of this in his many blog writing
sessions.

His truck, his books, and his words remain.
They will always be passed on.
For the thing we all learned most from him,
Was to always appreciate the words in every
single song.

The song that play when you hurt,
The one that plays when you are sad,
The one that plays when you are happy,
And all of the ones that remind us of dad.

Stick That in Your Poem and Smoke It!

So I knew this would be the title,
But then had no idea what to write.
So stick that in your poem and smoke it...
Goodnight.

His Black of Night

I sit in the black of night
To put the paper to the pencil
I write whatever comes to mind
Sitting in the black of night